Other books by Alan Pickard

How Reading is Learned

Storytime with Daddy

Listening to Children Read

Storytime with Mummy

Listening to Children Read

A *Handbook for Parents and Teaching Support Staff*

Alan Pickard

This edition first published in paperback by
Michael Terence Publishing in 2023
www.mtp.agency

Copyright © 2023 Alan Pickard

Alan Pickard has asserted the right to be identified as
the author of this work in accordance with the
Copyright, Designs and Patents Act 1988

ISBN 9781800945630

No part of this publication may be reproduced, stored
in a retrieval system, or transmitted, in any form or
by any means, electronic, mechanical, photocopying,
recording or otherwise, without the prior
permission of the publisher

Cover images
Dvulikaia | Abhisheksah99 | Kkornnphoto | Ddenisfilm
www.123rf.com

Cover design
Copyright © 2023 Michael Terence Publishing

Dedication

To children who love to read!

Contents

Preface 1

1: Stories from the classroom 5

2: A story about storytelling 20

3: The utterances of 6 year olds 24

4: Children reading world 32

5: Connecting with the year ones 37

6: More than meets the eye 40

7: A child's perspective 44

8: The state of literacy in the UK 51

Epilogue 59

Appendix 61

About the Author 63

Preface

It was during the second Covid pandemic lockdown when I was looking for a suitable project that I became interested in the idea of going into a local primary school and helping with children's reading. Although I managed to begin this in February 2022, it was halfway through the academic year, due to waiting for schools to be comfortable having volunteers back in school.

Whilst I was waiting to get started, I spent two or three months reading up on the subject of learning to read and I then decided to write a book called How Reading is Learned, which was published by an American firm in February 2023.

I had not planned to write another book on the subject, but because of my activities in more than one primary school I realised that I had accumulated a fair amount of experience in a school environment and I also experienced many interesting and useful observations. These consisted of seeing the advances in reading skills of individual children.

The first school I attended I was able to listen to reading from an age range of 5 to 9 year olds. This was not particularly structured, but it did give me the opportunity to cover a significant range of reading ages. I have described these experiences in the book and then taken it a bit further by describing various other aspects of reading with children.

Being a volunteer reader in a primary school is a very straightforward description and accurate, but I discovered that there was a lot more to it than I expected. Although it could be treated very straightforwardly, simply listening to one child after another reading from his or her given book and correcting their mistakes and so on, I decided very early on that my place was not to teach. Indeed, although I had read two or three excellent books on the subject, I had no intention of getting into the technicalities such as phonics, split digraphs and so on, not least because it may conflict with what and how the children have been taught.

I did not expect, nor was I involved in, any kind of assessment of the children's reading skills, apart from making one or two comments in their reading diary. These comments and my approach as far as I was concerned, had the purpose of simply encouraging the child's reading improvements.

Although I was given free rein, in the sense that I could choose which children to listen to, from a class list and wherever possible tried to concentrate on those who needed more help, I was also able to listen to good and even exceptionally good readers. This was, I believe beneficial to them because rather than them being ignored or left to their own devices, I felt it was useful to encourage them also. In my view, I was not only helping poor or struggling readers, but I felt that I was effectively coaching the more proficient ones. The fact that I went in not one, but two afternoons per week but was attached to one class of 6/7 year olds, enabled me to achieve a reasonable 'turnover' of some 27 children. I don't believe that my input would have been as effective if I only did one afternoon per week.

As can be seen in various chapters throughout this book I was able to get a great deal of insight and even inspiration from what I observed when listening to individual children reading to me. I also gained an insight into the operation and interaction of a complete class of children and as each week went by I got to know them a little bit better, albeit via only five to ten minute sessions. And I also learned all of their names!

26 March 2023

1
Stories from the classroom

Previous classroom experience consisted of helping in a primary school when my two daughters were at that age. I remember doing a demonstration of a small educational robot vehicle which I was reviewing for a magazine. I think that the most interesting part for the class was when I showed them that I could stand on top of it without it breaking. It was a very robust robot!

On another occasion I did an introductory Shakespeare 'workshop' for an older group. They may not have been expecting this to be exciting but when they realised that I was handing out printed sheets containing Shakespearean insults, they could not wait to participate. They all had a turn at calling each other obscure names and putting in the required amount of energy...

Not so long ago I was helping in a pre-school class of which my 4 year old granddaughter was a member. When the teacher asked me to read one of the children a story, I was pleased to do this. Out of the corner of my eye, I noticed another child showing an interest and she came and sat alongside, presumably to satisfy her curiousity. And then another and then another. Not exactly the Pied Piper, but I was delighted by this response and I was looking forward to getting involved in this activity again, as soon as possible.

***

Tuesday 25 January 2022

At last, I was able to visit a local primary school to help with children's reading. I spent an enjoyable and satisfying hour and a half listening to six 6 year olds reading for me, for five to ten minutes each. The children were not only well behaved, but cooperative and I would say pleased to read aloud from their chosen book.

After spending much time reading on the subject of reading and learning to read, I found it very interesting to see the process in action. Each child had reached a certain level of reading for their year group, but of course their actual reading and comprehension were all slightly different. I was particularly interested to see how, when a difficult word was encountered, unless they came to a stop, perhaps when this particular word had not been encountered previously, they would try and guess the word. I feel now that I understand that this is an essential part of learning to read.

One thing that I liked was that more than one of the children interacted with the illustrations and where they were already part way through reading their book, took the trouble to point out to me what had gone before. A very clear demonstration that reading was being enjoyed.

This first encounter as a reading volunteer was well up to expectations, a new experience for me, but in a way a consolidation of my commitment to reading and writing from a personal point of view.

Tuesday 1 February 2022

More of the same in one sense, but one different child. Interesting to meet the others again and confident that they would read as well as they could. Not disappointed, but I noticed the 'new' boy was very chatty and confident. His choice of book was 'The Wedding' and he not only engaged with the story and told me about a wedding he and his younger sister had attended, but his reading speed and ability was not as good as the others. I suspected that one of the reasons was that he was not focussing fully on the task in hand and I would process this later, especially if I was able to listen to him read on a subsequent occasion.

My initial perspective when embarking on this activity - helping children to improve their reading by me listening and correcting as we went along, was fine by me. I saw it as me making an appearance and simply being a pair of hands in the classroom environment. Not a problem as far as I was concerned, but although each child was sent along to me for reading aloud 'practice' and the teacher was selecting them, I had no idea why. What I was doing had almost no structure, but no doubt as the weekly visits went by I would get more of an insight.

As previously, I thoroughly enjoyed listening, but also observing the concentration and the willingness of the children to apply themselves to their reading. I found it gratifying to see learning taking place and at the same time realising that these 6 year olds had of course already learned to read, but would hopefully go on to improve and also become keen readers.

Tuesday 8 February 2022

Five more 6 year olds, ready and willing to read aloud from their chosen book. Another enjoyable session, very little responsibility on my part, just observing these children seemingly enjoying reading their story and engaging with same at various levels. In their own ways, making progress in their reading skills and good if I am helping them along with something which should serve them well in life and also give them pleasure.

Tuesday 15 February 2022

This time, somehow I managed to listen to 8 children reading individually and noted that there were 4 girls and 4 boys. Although spending 5 to 10 minutes listening and helping with their reading, there is very little time for conversation, but I did discover that two of the boys, one of whom was having real difficulty with the basics compared to his peers, actually stated that they did not like reading!

Not something I obviously wanted to hear and gives me a little concern, due to my passion for reading and also learning to read with all of its benefits. However, it was interesting to observe on the ground as it were, the reality in an educational environment that not everyone desires to embrace every aspect!

Nevertheless, another enjoyable and worthwhile session for me and hopefully I was able to make some kind of impression and encouragement. This particular observation itself, interestingly, demonstrated to me how worthwhile it is for me to have a useful input for young children embarking on what is such an important journey.

Tuesday 1 March 2022

Eight children read to me and I enjoyed it as much or even more than previously. In a way it feels like a privilege to have one small person at a time sent to me and be able to spend 5-10 minutes listening to them grapple with what in a way is a life skill they have only recently acquired. And they continue to improve at various levels and in a way they are grappling with the process itself.

I find it quite fascinating to observe their progress literally word by word and it is very interesting to see a child occasionally struggling and sometimes guessing a word, whether it is similar to another, or not. For example, 'when' and 'then' can be confused and 'what' and 'that'. And sometimes they may guess a word (or even a phrase!) by cross referring to the illustration on the page. As I said, fascinating when you consider what is going on in a child's brain attempting (and succeeding) to make sense of what is on the printed page.

Also of interest, having done this for a few weeks, is the range of reading proficiency, mostly 6 year olds but one or two 5 year olds. And varying levels of commitment, although this being mainly high. Ditto for ability and desire to engage with what they are reading, sometimes commenting and bringing their imagination into the tale being told.

Tuesday 8 March 2022

This week was unusual in that the seven 'customers' were all ones I had seen before, at least once. Ages ranged from 5 to 7 and of course various levels of achieved fluency. One boy was particularly engaged in the story he was reading, clearly enjoyed reading aloud, but at the same time enjoying the story itself. Others need to fully concentrate on word recognition and pronunciation, but this is all part of the early stages of the reading adventure.

Another boy, aged 5, I noticed seemed to really enjoy the sounds of words and phrases and took pleasure in reading the whole phrase again, as if he had 'captured it! Two of the girls read very confidently at a good speed.

Tuesday 15 March 2022

Another slight change of format. I saw seven 8-9 year olds, none of them seen before and interestingly, all read from the same book - 'Dancing the Night Away', being an Oxford Reading Tree book, Level 11.

Interesting dealing with slightly older children and I was bemused that they seemed very interested in what 'level' they were at. And also interesting, that even though they expected the chosen book to be easy, it still presented a challenge as a reading out loud exercise. I observed that one girl in particular, obviously a keen reader, went far beyond the word by word reading, but read with appropriate inflexion, good use of punctuation and parentheses. Even though she read at a good speed it was as if she was planning the intonation, etc.

One boy seemed as if he wasn't interested but was then more than happy to read a second chapter.

Tuesday 22 March 2022

A mixture of 5½(!) to 7. A 7 year old boy read very fluently and confidently and was happy to read the whole 32 pages of the Fat Frog. The following 6 year old was a complete contrast, having a low reading age and read Doctor Duck letter by letter, with some difficulty. He did persevere however, but needs help to get to a basic level.

The next six year old needed to focus, but had good word recognition. The 5½ year old read very quickly and the following 6 year old was a good reader and clearly enjoyed reading at home and school.

The last three boys all read Rock Pools which they seemed to find very interesting and easy to relate to.

Tuesday 29 March 2022

The first little girl, a 5 year old, seemed a little wound up, although she had read for me previously. She seemed unwilling at first, but I now realise that you may not know what is going on in their heads, or what may have occurred in the classroom. And there could always be tiredness to consider. All okay, but cooperation at a low level.

The next boy had good word recognition, but needed a bit of a push. The next one (5½), read very quickly, so needs a harder book next time.

The next 5 year old girl's reading ability was astounding. Very confident and word recognition was excellent.

A 6 year old whom I had seen previously, plodded, but needed to focus more.

Another very confident 5¾(!) girl. Age being a very important attribute I have now also realised. Clearly thoroughly enjoyed reading.

Last one. This boy read steadily and was conversational about the book content (Our Planet). Good word recognition.

Due I believe to some staff restrictions and a requirement for testing processes going on, I was asked if I minded doing some testing. This involved asking the individual child to go through a previously prepared quantity of words which they knew (or did not know) and their record being updated as to how many new words they now knew since the last test.

The words were in two categories, one being described as decoding where they could work out the word letter by letter if necessary and the other category was 'tricky'. This being a test of whether they could quickly recognise words immediately.

All of the children were able to show improvement in terms of the quantity of new words which they could now recognise, from three months earlier. Quite a wide range of ability for these mainly 6 year olds and significant improvements noted. Of the ten children I saw, two of the girls had already a very good record of word recognition and at this point they completed all of the words on the sheets.

My impression was that all of the children seemed to enjoy the process, almost as if it was a game and competitive in the sense that they saw it as an achievement. And many of the children clearly enjoyed reading and indicated that they read their own books at home.

Tuesday 4 April 2022

Testing. A problem with getting (reading) testing, I was asked to help with that. Each of ten children went through their previous word sheets and were seen to recognise most or all of the words that they did not know about three months ago. They all seemed to enjoy this exercise and of course it was a confidence booster, especially for one or two who now knew all of the words and obviously realised this.

Tuesday 26 April 2022

Always interesting to observe the variation of ability, sometimes regardless of age. One boy seemed very nervous and ill at ease, but soon got into his stride and began to discuss the story he was reading. An 8 year old seemed to have a lower reading age, but cooperated fully. Another 8 year old was a slow reader, but having seen him before I noticed and told him that he was improving.

Tuesday 10 May 2022

Listening to young children reading is endlessly fascinating at many levels. This week the oldest child was 8 and the youngest was 6. Each one cooperated and one child in particular asked me if he could read all four of his books! This was not possible due to time constraints and the suggested limit of no more than 5 minutes. However, always good to see a definite liking for not only reading, but reading aloud. Another 6 year old was very engaged and particularly interested in the process of reading and had a clear interest in words themselves. Another 6 year old not only read his level 9 book well, but almost insisted he wanted to read past halfway and in fact the full 32 pages, which he did.

Although I am not and was not involved in the preliminary teaching of reading for these children, I have the pleasure of observing their application and endeavours in trying to improve their reading and vocabulary. I know that they have been taught to deal with an unknown word letter by letter and sounding until they get the difficult word right.

The main fascination for me is seeing the actual process of learning to read as described in textbooks, with my own eyes (and ears!).

Tuesday 17 May 2022

Five children listened to this week and my observations are confined to the interesting and amusing comments that children of this age (8 to 9 year olds) make, particularly of their own volition.

One little girl reading the words 'drama queen' just had to tell me about her 7 year old sister who was just that. Another girl informed me that the reason her reading was interrupted the previous week was that her brother was ill at school and they therefore had to go home early. But apparently this was a false alarm and he wasn't actually ill at all! And the third girl, being very confident, would have liked to have talked more about the story, rather than merely reading out loud!

One of the two boys was very serious and needed to tell me that he had a tendency to ignore full stops and had a problem with certain difficult words. He did however read very well, was confident and engaged and I did get him to admit that he read well.

The next boy seemed to be struggling with the book he had brought, but it was clearly a high level reader and contained some very difficult words which he attempted very well. Very impressive application and possibly someone who would be very driven.

The last reader was clearly very keen and read competently and I learned that she had lots of books on cats.

Being involved with young children reading aloud is interesting at so many levels, not least when they provide their unsolicited and individual comments around their reading experience.

Tuesday 24 May 2022

This time a more general observation. A selection of children aged around 6, four boys and one girl. Each one a good standard of reading for their age and my impression being that they were quite happy to come along and read aloud.

A bit of a cliché to say how fascinating it is to listen to the comments which children of this age come out with, but there are amusing instances, such as one of the boys part way through the reading, took a small soft toy (a monkey) out of his pocket, put it on the table and announced that he would help with his reading. However, this particular boy is a very good reader and also a keen one.

Having only around five minutes per child does not provide opportunity for much conversation outside of the reading exercise, but I enjoy the fact that they bring their mummy or daddy into the reading process and remark on which are their parents' favourite animals for example, or subjects. Or will volunteer anything from their experience which ties in with the story they are reading.

Some of the children at this age exhibit pride in what they do, such as the little girl who immediately informed me that she had moved from reading level 6 to level 7. If they are given a task such as going back to their classroom and asking their teacher to send the next reader, you can see the concentration on their face as they leave. Sometimes they 'deliver' the child to me and occasionally will suggest who to send to the Reading Area!

A particular pleasure is when the individual child does not take exception (usually the case) to being corrected and often show pleasure in getting the word right and even repeating the whole phrase or sentence. Another one is where they are concentrating either very hard on going along word by word, or in the case of more fluent reading they will show their amusement in the story events, which of course proves that they are taking in what they are reading.

A worthwhile occupation for me and hopefully increasing the child's confidence, perhaps not just in reading, but makes the experience for me very rewarding.

Tuesday 7 June 2022

Five children read to me, all of whom I had seen before. Each one completely cooperating, but one girl last time was very pleased with herself as she had gone up a reading level. Interestingly, she had to work hard with her 'Australian Adventure' book, which contained several difficult words. I considered that she needed to perhaps focus more.

Another boy had to go back to class, but I should see him next week – and find out why he had produced a very easy book to read!

Tuesday 14 June 2022

Six children, aged from 6 to 8 years. All seen previously, some maybe three or four times. Whenever I ask if they enjoy reading aloud and being listened to, they all seem very positive.

Interestingly at least one or two read very well, so I can only presume that they find it beneficial.

Tuesday 21 June 2022

Just like adults, children can be contrary and inconsistent. One 9 year old effectively volunteered to be a reader when I visited the classroom. She read well, with great energy. When I pointed out that she should slow down, she happily re-read the last paragraph, just as I asked.

When I asked her if she enjoyed reading aloud – she said no! And that she did not like reading, but did read at home ….

I am sure that she will do very well in school and no doubt achieve great things.

2
A story about storytelling

After spending some twenty weeks of afternoon sessions at a local primary school, listening to individual children reading to me, each for five minutes or so, last week I was able to perform the function of storyteller to three separate classes of 5 to 7 year olds. Each session was no more than twenty minutes and I told three stories which I had previously written. Each story was about a bird which had got itself into trouble. After each story I asked the children if they had had any experience of the story content.

Having some involvement over the years helping in school, doing various talks on different educational subjects and my experience as a lecturer in higher education, I had no particular apprehension about doing the storytelling sessions. Interestingly, the sessions went according to plan and it was a great pleasure to literally have twenty-five to thirty children sat at my feet and hanging on my every word! It was almost a textbook situation and because I told the stories, not read them, I was able to see their faces and note their interest.

The most surprising thing was the enthusiasm of several of the children in each class, wanting to share their experiences and a few of them were keen to engage more than once. This meant that I had to actually manage the situation in terms of turn taking and timing.

The other surprise was that the next two sessions (I did one after another), produced virtually the same experience.

***

I thoroughly enjoyed the listening to children read experience even more than I expected to. I also found it particularly interesting, having read various books on the subject of learning to read, to see the process in action as individual children applied themselves to the task of dealing with vocabulary, spelling, pronunciation and of course word recognition. One thing that was very evident was how each child is different and develops in different ways in this respect, namely learning to read.

The storytelling sessions were most enjoyable and I would certainly like to do more of that and realised that I would have to dig out some of my stories and indeed write some more, with whichever age group is concerned. This activity maybe complements the reading activities, but if I had a preference it would be for listening to reading, not least as this is a one to one tailored activity.

(The story I told can be read in the Appendix.)

***

In September I was hoping to attend two different local primary schools, but it is interesting to note that it has been a real struggle getting this activity up and running. Partly due to the effects of Covid and before February of this year, it would have been impossible to get into a school, but even since then it is extremely difficult getting a response, or even an acknowledgement. Then I contacted a school and of course informed them that I have a DBS and that I am already carrying out this activity. Sending an email initially, then following up with a telephone call usually resulted in no actual response. Exceptions are when I have spoken to one headteacher and was awaiting confirmation for September and another headteacher sent me an excellent email reply and confirmation that I would be welcome in September. Hopefully this would result in having these two schools on my list. I would also be happy to do storytelling if they would like that.

***

If I was telling this 'story' perhaps one of the most amazing aspects is that I have carried out twenty children reading sessions, listened to approximately sixty different children between 5 and 9 years old and then done three storytelling sessions to something like seventy or eighty children in total. Literally none of this would have occurred if I had not organised it.

I am quite bemused by the fact that apart from speaking to the school secretary and liaising with three teaching assistants, I have been the driver of this situation, mainly by turning up every week and effectively asking the children to be sent to me for reading. The deputy head who is responsible for reading at the school I have had email correspondence with, but never met. The headteacher has said hello to me a couple of times, but I was never introduced.

To conclude, I am very pleased and feel a sense of achievement in what I have been able to do over the last several months and I look forward to continuing at least with what I have been doing so far. Attending two schools per week would be very satisfying, particularly as the schools are then able to make use of my assistance, within their busy timetable. The latter causing them to be so fully occupied that it seems either difficult or impossible for them to import the help they clearly need.

3
The utterances of 6 year olds

During the first term at a 'new' school, I was occasionally amused by comments made by the twenty-five 6 year olds whom I listened to reading every week. I did not record these each week, but I thought I would write some down before I forgot about them, or at least forgot to chronicle them.

One little girl who was keen to apply herself to the task of reading aloud is making steady progress and is enthusiastic in her reading. Often in the school books they are provided with on a continuous basis, although they are aimed at 6/7 year olds (Key Stage 2), they are often confronted with some fairly difficult and/or unfamiliar words, which can grind them to a halt. In particular, forenames and surnames can be very difficult and I don't exactly encourage them with these words and sometimes disregard them as they are not common enough to be committed to memory. However, although the children may be happy to be told how to say a particular word, sometimes it is as if they just don't know what to do with the difficult word. For example, how are they expected to process a word like 'Achilles'?

One particular girl came to a stop when the word Zephyr appeared. I told her how to say it and then when it occurred again she tried, but was still a bit baffled by it, clearly being outside of her phonic experience. I got her to repeat it after me and then when it occurred on the next page she pronounced it correctly, which we were both amused by. She then said, 'Do you know I have had problems with that all week!' This of course made me laugh, because I would not describe her as a drama queen, but I liked her sense of humour.

In another week, a girl who was a particularly good reader, not only read fluently, but with inflection. But then the dreaded unfamiliar proper noun, which in this case was the girl's name Sinead, stopped her in her tracks. Again, I pronounced and told her it was an Irish name. Next time it occurred, she was still not getting it. So I said to her just think of the 'sin' part being 'shin' and the 'ead' part being like lemonade. She then pronounced it perfectly, complete with my northern accent (in a Gloucestershire school). Although she was slightly puzzled, I pointed out to her that she probably would remember that name and she may remember that she made me laugh.

This week I had already heard a little boy read to me, but later on, just as I was about to listen to the next child, he had appeared to my left in the corner, where there was a book case and when I asked him if he was supposed to be there and shouldn't he be back in the classroom, he said that the teacher said he could look at these books. At this I point I asked the next girl if she was okay with her classmate sitting there while she read to me. She was not fazed by this at all. He had already pointed out that this encyclopaedic volume he was looking through had a picture of Mary Shelley and lots of other characters from history. Just before I started listening to his classmate, he told me he was looking in the book to see what he could do when he was grown up. And then he politely asked me what I was going to do when I grow up! Not batting an eyelid, I said to him that I would like to be a writer. He then told me that he had found a writer in the book.

Generally speaking, I have no problem dealing with these children and they are almost all very polite and cooperative. However, occasionally a child will tell me that they don't actually like reading, either when I have asked the question, or not. As to be expected in a year group there is quite a range of reading capability and in their attitudes towards reading. Once I had a little boy who produced four books and asked me if he could read them all to me. Others will announce that they are only going to read two or four pages whatever, which I usually ignore. Some of the very keen readers, if I ask them if they would like to continue will say yes, or perhaps indicate that they have had enough. Then there are those who will ask, or even inform me that they are going to read to the end of the book. These are usually picture books with text, which they may be part way through, but the page size could be 24 or even 32. In other words, the children quite often negotiate, or try to negotiate up or down with the number of pages to be read. Whilst there is no point in me insisting on a particular number of pages, depending on the child and the book, I simply use my judgement in each case.

On the downside, where a child may be less cooperative than usual, there is no point in me taking it personall,y or even thinking of not listening to that child read, because one of the main reasons I do this work is to encourage and persuade children of the vital importance of reading in their whole life. But at 6 years old this is not really a conversation you can have and there is no point in any kind of lecturing approach.

Sadly, in this situation (bearing in mind that I am not in a teaching or assessment role), all that I can do is to encourage reading and wherever possible make it an interesting, enjoyable and sometimes an amusing experience.

***

Turning up at school two afternoons every week, giving up my time and putting in a fair amount of effort with young children's reading as effectively as I can, is appreciated by the school, the class teacher and I believe most of the children. But in one sense, the pleasure is all mine. As this is something I can fit into my weekly activities and is something that I love to do, because of my lifelong interest in reading, writing and of course literature, it is, to coin a phrase, just up my street. Apart from my working life spent in industry, education, accountancy and spare time writing, I have always been fascinated by words, the printed and spoken word, wordplay and so on. This leads me to believe that I am very suited to doing this kind of work and although it can be quite intense listening to 6 year olds for 5 to 10 minutes at a time, poring over words, correcting and sometimes explaining, it can be quite tiring. But this has no effect whatsoever on my wishing to continue this activity indefinitely.

I titled one of my previous websites as 'Writing for Pleasure' and of course it follows that inherent in that phrase is 'reading for pleasure', but also listening to reading, for pleasure. And of course there is the satisfaction in knowing that you may be having an influence on children who are learning to read. And the age group I am engaged with (currently 6 year olds), many of them are at the beginning of reading and indeed struggling, but at the same time I can observe them improving and realising that they are improving. Another satisfaction is when they tell me about books that they are reading outside of school and of course this demonstrates that it is their choice.

***

Another benefit for me is having studied the learning to read process to an extent, it is quite fascinating to listen and observe young children reading aloud. There are many instances which I have recognised from my reading on the subject. To see it actually occur, for example the words 'What' and 'That' (with a leading capital letter) can be mixed up by a child, it being something to do with the similar shape of the word. But the point is that it is possible to see what you have read in action. Another interesting occurrence is confusion between 'b' and 'd'. This of course will be overcome, but it is interesting to observe this is not as clear as it is to us experienced readers.

Yet another, what I describe as a side benefit, is the behaviour and personalities of the children. At the time of writing (in my case I am currently associated with a class of twenty-six 6 year olds). Although I am quite happy to listen to children read from 5 years old and upwards, I am very content to be 'specialising in' 6 year old readers. Over the weeks I get to know the children more as individuals and this is indeed what they are. In a classroom situation they are expected to conform in many ways, but in practice their individual personalities are developing, along with their confidence. In my view these 'second years' are realising that they have graduated from being 'first years'. I have been told by the class teacher that they benefit from reading to as many adults as possible. Although I do not have the opportunity for any kind of lengthy conversations with them, I do get to interact from time to time, especially when I have to respond to their comments or questions.

Some children will tell me about their siblings, or their pets, or places they have visited, especially things arising from the stories they are reading. Sometimes they will give opinions on the content of the characters in the story, point things out to me and sometimes their enthusiasm drifts into the pictures in their book whilst they are reading. Or they will stop reading and study the pictures.

Generally I find these children to be well behaved and cooperative although it is amusing that a child will begin by not sitting properly on the chair, or be moving about or obscuring the page with their head! Of course, as they get more used to me they can see how far they can go, for instance announcing that they only want to read two pages, or 'can I stop now?', or 'I will read two more pages', or 'I will read to the end of the book so that I can have a new book', etc. Whichever way you look at it, in my mind they are engaging in the wonderful learning to read process and being connected with books and what they can give them.

When I have finished listening to one child I ask them to send the next one to me when they go back into the classroom. Almost without exception, this is something that they basically enjoy doing, probably because it is a responsibility that they have been given, not to mention being able to tell a fellow class classmate to do something! Apart from the fact that occasionally one of them may forget to deliver the message. Often when a child is passing by and I am listening to reading, or just finishing, they will ask me who is next. One boy did this twice and when I asked him if he was volunteering (to read) he said 'No I just want to know who's next!' But my suspicion is that he wants to be able to go into the classroom and tell a child that he or she will be next! Could this be some kind of empowerment?

Another amusement is that when one of the children comes out of the classroom having been given permission to go to the toilet, on their return I notice some dawdling and looking down the corridor at what might be going on in the school hall. Thus maximising their release from the classroom, this is no doubt something which they will continue to apply throughout their schooling...

The antics of 6 year olds I find to be generally entertaining, interesting and often amusing.

4
Children reading world

Today it was my turn to read to Mr Pickard and when I went over to see him I told him that I knew my book was in the box because I remembered to bring it. I told him that the day before I had left my book at home, but I told him that it was such a relief yesterday when I found out that he not was coming in that day. Mr Pickard laughed out loud, he thought that was very funny and I wonder if he thinks that I am a bit of a drama queen? When we were reading the story it was a book about a gran getting a new car. I kept saying Grandma but Mr Pickard said it was 'Gran' and I told him that I was saying it because my gran was called Grandma. And I told him that my Grandma's car was white.

On the afternoons where some of us read to Mr Pickard, he sits at a table outside the classroom and he starts off by asking for someone on his list. When a boy or girl has finished reading to Mr Pickard he tells them which one to ask for next. We put our book and diary back in the big book box and then we go and tell the next boy or girl it is their turn.

Some of us try to find out who is next and one of the boys asked Mr Pickard twice who was next and he said to him, 'Why, are you volunteering?' He said 'No I just wanted to know.' I wonder if Mr Pickard thinks he was being nosy! Some of the children ask Mr Pickard if they can read next and he tells them that they might be able to later on, or the next time he comes in. Some of the children ask him if they can read, even if they've read the day before.

I like reading to Mr Pickard, because it is interesting reading out loud and it makes you try harder to get the words right. Sometimes I try to emphasise the words when someone in the story is speaking. Once I got a bit too excited and I spoke the words too loudly. Mr Pickard didn't seem to mind, I think he thought it was funny.

***

When I started reading to Mr Pickard at the beginning, I didn't really want to do it. And I told him that I didn't like reading and I would rather play video games. Mr Pickard seemed to ignore what I said and I had to read a few pages of my book. But I knew that I would have to do this again, probably next week. I think I am getting better at reading and perhaps it is not so bad after all. Mr Pickard told me that reading was very important and he did say to me once that I would be able to read books on all sorts of things including books on video games! He said to me that next time I was in a toy shop I could look for books on video games. I think my reading is getting better and some of the story books are quite interesting.

I think Mr Pickard was very surprised when I asked him if I was reading one day and he said to me that I had already read the day before, so I would have to wait until next week. I was a bit disappointed.

***

I think I am a good reader, especially as I am only 6. I like reading and I like reading to Mr Pickard, because I usually have a book which I am enjoying reading and I like to do the voices and read the story properly. Mr Pickard says it is inflection. I don't think I could spell that but I might recognise it if I see it in a book.

***

Every time it is my turn to read to Mr Pickard, I tell him I have left my book and reading diary at home. He tells me to get a suitable book from the bookcase, but he always says the book is too easy because I am a good reader and I can read quickly. Last week he found a copy of a book called Encyclopaedia Britannica and I was reading from that. I said it was easy but he pointed out that there were a lot of words I had to be helped with. Mr Pickard said I should ask my teacher for a harder book.

***

I like reading to Mr Pickard. This week I had my reading diary, but I couldn't find my book so Mr Pickard told me to choose one from the bookcase. The book was called The Magic Pantomime and it was quite hard, with some pictures, but a lot of words. I really enjoyed reading this and I liked the story. When Mr Pickard asked me if I had read enough I said no, so that I could read some more pages. I noticed that the book had 42 pages and I would have liked to read all of the book, but Mr Pickard said there wasn't enough time, although I had read all of Chapter 1. He said that I should take the book home with me and read all of it.

***

I read for Mr Pickard today, but later on I went over to the table where he was sitting ready for the next reader and I was looking in the corner of the bookcase at some books. Mr Pickard said 'Aren't you supposed to be in the classroom?' I said that the teacher told me that I could come and have a look at these books. At this point the next girl arrived to read to Mr Pickard and he asked her if it was okay that he was reading that book while she are reading to him. She said yes, it was okay. Before they started, I said to Mr Pickard that this book was very interesting because it had famous people in it and one of them was called Mary Shelley. Mr Pickard said that she wrote the Frankenstein book. I told Mr Pickard that I was looking at all these different people because I was wondering what I would do when I grew up. I asked Mr Pickard what he would do when he grew up. Mr Pickard replied, 'I think I would like to be a writer.' Then I told him that I had found a writer in this book.

***

Today I am reading to Mr Pickard and the book I am reading has some difficult words in it and I think they are called proper nouns and they are like the names of people which I have never heard of. One of the words was Zephyr. I had no idea really what to do with it. Mr Pickard told me how to pronounce it and next time it came up I tried but I was still puzzled by it. Next time it occurred Mr Pickard got me to say it two or three times and then I was saying it correctly. I said to Mr Pickard, 'Do you know, I have been having a problem with that all week!'

***

The book I am reading does not have many pictures. Mr Pickard said that I was a very good reader for that reason. One or two words I find difficult are usually people's names. This book was called Sinead the Firewoman. When I saw the name Sinead it was as if I didn't know what to do with it. I tried to pronounce it twice, but when it came up again Mr Pickard said to me, 'Imagine the 'sin' is shin and the 'ead' is like in lemonade. So it is like saying shin ade - Sinead.' So I said it right and when I'd finished reading, Mr Pickard said, 'You said that correctly, but you will remember that word, because you made me laugh.' I was puzzled, but Mr Pickard said, 'You said it exactly as I told you to, but using my northern accent!'

5
Connecting with the year ones

Having settled myself in to the routine of listening to the Year 2 class for nearly two and a half terms I discovered that for the rest of the term this class would be doing swimming! I then offered to listen to children from the classroom next door, namely a Year 1 class comprising 5 to 6 year olds. I had already listened to a few of these children previously when the other class was not available. Although I would have been more than happy to continue both afternoons with Year 2, but as this situation occurred I realised that it would be nice to spend time with the younger ones. And of course as I had offered to continue next school year these Year 1s would become the Year 2s which I expected to be involved with then. So a win win situation, apart from seeing less of the Year 2 children.

When I contacted the Year 1 teacher I suggested that I would like to meet the class and that if she was happy for me to tell them a story by way of introduction, I would be happy to do so.

This occurred and all went well. When I entered the classroom the children were being primed by their teacher and instructed to assemble on to the carpet. I believe this was also a means of calming the children down as they had just come in from the playground. I sat myself down in front of some 25 or so children (me sat on a small chair, not on the carpet!). I could see that the children were certainly anticipating something of a different experience, namely about to listen to a story from Mr Pickard.

I told the story of the Hen in Trouble which I wrote many years ago, having included it in a children's storybook, but before that I had read it to my three grandchildren. This is one of the stories on my website and also as a recording on my YouTube channel. The story is short and probably took three or four minutes to tell, but I could see that it was well received and one or two of the children asked for another story. Another said he would like to hear it again. Unfortunately, that had not been planned, so it was now time to start listening to one child at a time reading to me, until the end of school that afternoon.

Although I have listened to a small number of children from this class reading previously, this was the first time that I would be working my way through the full list. This will last for the rest of this summer term and I'm expecting to continue with this class next year, when they become Year 2. And for the rest of this term I will continue on Wednesday afternoons with the current Year 2 class.

It will be interesting to begin again with Year 2 in September, having already established a relationship with this class during the present term.

In my experience, primary school children from the age of five to nine almost without exception, enjoy being listened to when they read aloud. This Year 1 class is no exception and as well as enjoying the one to one experience, they seem to be in no doubt about the benefits of reading, presumably because they can see the advantage of being able to learn more words and move onto the next book. They are mostly interested in going to the next level. Unless they have been brainwashed or lectured to, it is as if they actually realise the importance of being able to read as well as possible. Most or all of them seem to know that they can get pleasure from reading and in particular if there is any humour, intentional or otherwise, when reading their books and sometimes they seem to appreciate word play.

One little boy said to me, 'I want to be like you, a good reader, but I want to be a footballer!' An interesting take, but I wonder if the fact that someone comes in to read with his class every week, underlines its significance in their minds? I certainly get the impression that I am taken seriously and made to feel welcome by the children.

6

More than meets the eye

If someone saw me sat near the classroom with a 5 or 6 year old child reading to me they may think that the child is reading aloud and I am observing and correcting, as the book was read from. This is of course true, but from my perspective I am not just listening and watching the child read, but in a sense it is as if I can see 'the cogs' going round in the child's brain.

Some time before I began listening to children from Year 1 and Year 2 classes, the child had previously been taught to read, either in a reception class, or via their parents teaching them rudimental reading, beginning with the letters of the alphabet and so on.

I am seeing the results of this learning process and as the weeks go by I see improvements in word recognition, pronunciation and seeing a child understanding what they are reading, including in the context of looking at the pictures in the book which they are reading.

I do not consider it is my place to get involved in the technical aspects of learning to read and possibly confuse a child in the process, in respect of how they have actually learned the basic reading process. Also, I am not teaching them or assessing them, but my primary aim is to encourage them, especially if the opportunity for realising enjoyment of reading occurs.

There are many things going on when a child reads and of course this becomes more transparent if they are reading aloud. In my experience, I would say that somehow the children like to read out loud, as they must realise that improving reading skills is very important and something they wish to improve on. My view is that at the age of 5 or 6, or even 7, it would be pointless to try and lecture a child on the benefit of reading and that it is preferable for them to discover this for themselves. Another factor which aids this process, is that if they belong to a busy class of thirty children, they relish the idea of having any kind of one to one experience, in this case with an alternative grown up.

I have observed children reading letter by letter and sometimes struggling with that. As they improve and accumulate more and more words which they recognise easily and quickly, they then progress to reading word by word in a fairly mechanical way. The next stage is for them to read in a slightly more fluent way, which then needs to improve, including taking notice of punctuation.

Reading speed improves slowly, but maybe not a lot of interest is being taken in what they are reading. In other words, they are literally reading word by word by word and in some cases clearly enjoying this process. This gives me pleasure because even if they are not reading fluently, they are now becoming more expert at recognising and pronouncing words correctly and of course building up their vocabulary.

Being a writer, but only having very small amount of time with each child, I try to listen to as many children as possible in less than two hours. The most I can manage is twelve. But I also try to get them to read as many words as possible. In other words, (again, as a writer), I am looking at a word count!

The next thing I often notice is that they begin to read more fluently, but also using inflection. Then there are those who realise that speech marks enable a change of tone, just as an exclamation mark allows them to raise their voice!

In a way, seeing a 7 year old reading very well, there is a point where you notice that they are actually looking ahead at the next word or two. I was very interested to see this, because the child's brain is learning or has learned to plan ahead in their reading and of course particularly as they are reading aloud. In a way I am assuming they have not been taught to do this and it is some kind of instinctive process which they are utilising, obviously without realising they are doing it.

Wherever possible I will complement a child on a particularly good effort, but without being patronising or condescending. One of the things I do like to say to the child, in what I just described, is that they have read very well and that I could actually listen to them reading that book to me without me looking at what they are reading. To me this is a major step forward if they can read out loud to another person with such accuracy that the sense of what they are reading is conveyed. And in effect, the child is reading me a story!

I find there are many amusing instances. such as when a child comes to a word which they really have no knowledge of and are unable to make sense of it. They do what they probably do when they are reading on their own, which is to guess a word they think it might be. This is very amusing (to me), especially when the word they choose makes no sense of what the word is or should be.

Time does not usually permit, but I occasionally have a conversation about how easy it is to read silently and how difficult or how much more hard work it is to read out loud. And of course it takes longer. Most of the brighter children I come across completely understand this and it is amazing sometimes that you can have a conversation with a child reading, about reading!

7
A child's perspective

The first school I attended for the purpose of listening to children read, I thoroughly enjoyed and at the end of the school year I would have been prepared to continue one afternoon per week. I did however, have the opportunity of continuing this activity nearer to my home, as we had moved house. The nearest school to where I lived was much closer and if necessary was within walking distance. Although I was prepared to do this listening activity two sessions per week and even if this was in two different schools, because I said I was available to operate like this, the school I approached was happy for me to go there for both sessions.

The headteacher responded to my email enquiry very positively and said that he would be pleased for me to come to the school in September. As I still operate my part time business working from home, he said that he was happy to work around my schedule. I said that Tuesday and Wednesday afternoons would suit me and this modus operandi was established.

When I did the listening 'work' the previous year, I noticed that I felt that it was not enough to just do less than a couple of hours per week and of course this was for less than 40 weeks of the year, with a long summer holiday. Two sessions per week I thought would be ideal and provide a sense of continuity for me.

I had a meeting with the headteacher the week before I started. This was a useful introduction, as he told me about the school, went through safeguarding and various other admin aspects and he took me to meet the Year 2 class, which I was to be effectively attached to.

Whereas previously I had listened to children from the age of 5 years to 9 years old, which was very interesting, dealing with one year group of 6 to 7 year olds also appealed, as it meant that I would be able to concentrate on a (mere) 30 children and hopefully over the academic year get to know them and be able to observe individual progress. This indeed took place and at the time of writing I am now in the middle of the summer term.

Engaging in this kind of activity enables observation and discovery of the dynamics involved in reading out loud and listening to a child reading. In this chapter I am going to discuss how I perceive these children's perception of what may be going on in their heads.

On the one hand, I would like to think that my approach to doing this has a positive and beneficial effect on the children. That could sum up the entire situation in very simple terms. But I believe that there is much more going on in terms of those dynamics. I generally work from my list of names, but this is based on the list which the class teacher gave me initially. My list contains 28 names and I could split that into the children who need more time to get their reading level up to the required standard for their age group, then say a middle block who are doing quite well and also improving. And then there are a small number whose reading is at a very high standard and beyond their actual age. In other words, their reading age is much higher than that of a 7 year old, or possibly even one or two years higher.

I'm sure that primary school teachers are well aware of the extensive ability range within one year group and this presents problems with a class teacher having insufficient time to spend with individuals, especially the more needy ones.

It is a very simplistic comment to state that it is such a great activity to go into the school and in my case help with reading. Unfortunately this does not solve the fundamental problem of literacy in schools. On the one hand it proves or reinforces that there is a problem in providing the required level of encouragement. And on the other, that there is a shortage of people like me, or parents, or grandparents, etc either being available or perhaps not realising that they could get involved in this activity.

My view is that ironically the schools are understaffed and of course the class sizes are too large. When I set out to find a school or schools which would take up my offer, I found some of them very unresponsive. Some did not even respond to an email enquiry. Others said that they were interested but they did not follow through despite a second contact by email or telephone from me. I can only surmise that it would be another administrative burden to have someone come into the school from outside (despite the necessary DBS), but maybe a class teacher would possibly not relish having someone else around to organise, monitor or whatever. However, by its nature, it is very easy for someone like me to listen to one child after another for five minutes or so, with very little disruption to the classroom activity. I listen to a child from my list and when that child has read to me I simply ask them to go back to the class and give them a name of the next child to come and see me. Not only does this work very well and easily, but I know for a fact that the child relishes being able to go to the next child and instruct them!

Another observation I have is that the school I attend at the moment, I would say is a very pleasant environment with a good ethos, the children being very well behaved, polite and very willing to read to me. One teacher had told me that earlier on her class children were very excited about being able to read to me. Also she said that the children enjoy one to one and in particular being able to read to another grown up. I imagine that another reason for them liking to do this, is that it gives them a bit more confidence in being able to talk to someone who is not their teacher, or their parent and perhaps it makes them feel grown up (as a 6 or 7 year old).

Each time a child is requested for reading, I am fairly sure that as soon as they hear their name they instantly respond. I have noticed if I walk into the classroom to ask for the first child, they almost spring to attention, which of course is rather gratifying. But I used to wonder why they were so keen. That because surely they were not having this behaviour drummed into them. I also assume that I give them the impression (which I'm sure is correct), that they understand how important their reading and improving their reading is. Obviously, at reception level and prior to that they have been taught their alphabet and then enough words to make a start at being able to read. And they must get feedback in their own minds, as they are able to read more words, move up in reading levels and gain access to more books whether story or non-fiction.

***

I have another theory! That someone such as myself, who is somewhat an outsider from school, because I am coming into the school not once, but twice during the week, perhaps sends a message that reading has a special place in learning.

Obviously, stepping out of the classroom to read to me underlines its importance and of course is a diversion, or a novelty, compared to the usual classroom activity.

When the head teacher took me to meet the class and their teacher, he made a big thing of my coming into school and taking time to do this. Also the teacher told them I was not being paid, but coming in to do this because I liked doing it. The headteacher completed the introduction by emphatically telling the children that I was an author. He also added that 'He therefore knows what he is talking about!' I like to think that this could have made quite an impression with the children.

A number of times one of the children have asked me if I have written the book which they were reading and other questions about books. I have noticed that the children get quite concerned when the book which they are reading is damaged or worn, or the pages have become loose. A number of times I have shown them how the book is put together and they are always interested for some reason in the page numbering and very interested in how many pages they have read, especially when they want to finish a book (usually so they can choose the next book). They also like to tell me if they have gone up to the next level (colour coded) and will always tell me if it is their birthday!

***

As I mentioned earlier, going into school as a volunteer is considered to be very commendable. I know that the headteacher and the class teacher very much appreciate my coming in to school and spend my time with the children. Other people I speak to on my way to the classroom say hello and I can tell that my presence is approved of. Similarly, when I talk to friends and acquaintances about this they are impressed, not least because I am giving up my time. But I am sure that they do not realise how much I thoroughly enjoy doing this. Spending up to two hours in one session of listening to one child after another for at least 5 minutes can result in as many as 12 readings. This is quite intensive, especially going word by word through several pages in a picture or text book and it can be quite tiring. But it is an absolute pleasure not only dealing with and helping these young children, but for someone who has loved dealing with words for a very long time and the intellectual context of what I am doing, it is a great pleasure.

8
The state of literacy in the UK

When I started writing this book it was partly as a follow on from my How Reading is Learned book. The inspiration was mainly due to having now had more experience in the primary school environment, specifically listening to individual children reading, being in the age range of 5 to 7 years. This as well as being an account of experiences gained observing how children engage in their reading and also improvements they make. Over the weeks and recognising individual children, I am able to notice progress. At the same time I can see for myself many things which I have read about concerning learning to read.

Although it was never my intention to see how children are taught to read in state schools, unsurprisingly I have been able to observe just that. Before I got involved in studying the learning of reading, I had a general impression that literacy standards were not good generally.

The following statement from the readeasy.org.uk website, I found difficult to believe:

> 2.4 million adults in England alone can not read at all or struggle to read, but many people don't tell anyone.

There is clearly a problem with adult literacy in England! And no doubt elsewhere.

According to the U.S. Department of Education:

> 54% of U.S. adults 16-74 years old, about 130 million people, lack proficiency in literacy, reading below the equivalent of a sixth grade level. 9 Sept 2020.

In this day and age (the technological one) this particular educational level is concerning. This is rather disturbing if it is compared to other achievements such as say technology, engineering, science and so on, where both the UK and the US have achieved fantastic successes in various academic and industrial environments.

The ability to read to a good standard is fundamentally important and should not be neglected. Nor should the stated percentages be acceptable. Not being able to read well is literally a handicap and can prevent children, older children and students from not achieving their full potential in what may be their chosen field. Indeed they may never even know what their achievements could be, if they are cut off due to poor reading skills.

This situation is very concerning and like so many of areas in the UK which are underfunded, is detrimental to the intellectual and economic life of Britain. Everyone is aware of the problems with the NHS and there are other areas such as transport, climate change and so on. But I am focused on problems in education and in particular literacy. Because of my lifelong love of words, their meanings and what can be expressed with them, literacy, literature, reading and writing are extremely important to me. Hence my evangelical approach!

***

It is a well known fact that state schools and in particular primary schools, are underfunded in terms of equipment and possibly even books, but the main problem is surely that they have classes with as many as 30 children in them. This is a huge number for one teacher to be able to deal with, even with the help of teaching assistants. A figure of 18-24 has been suggested as a more reasonable range. During my reading experience this year, I was 'attached' to a Year 1 and a Year 2 class, both of which had exactly thirty children each (the maximum).

I have done this voluntary work in two different schools and I have previously been involved many years ago in two other primary schools, where I did classroom activity, but also was a parent governor in those two schools.

I am not carrying out research at all, so most of what I am talking about in this book is based on observation and is anecdotal rather than scientifically proven. But I would say that this does not mean it has no value. I have one or two impressions which I can mention and I imagine that anyone reading this book would recognise what I am say and not be inclined to disbelieve what I am suggesting.

The first consideration is that whereas I believe no one would state that class sizes are acceptable, but rather the opposite. But an individual primary school teacher has very little time available to listen to every child in the class read to them. I am sure that they will try and do their best to do this, but by definition, the class size prohibits this from occurring as much as it could. In my case I have not been aware of persons such as myself carrying out any listening or specific listening activities. Obviously, I am not a member staff and it is possible that there could be someone else in the building, especially as I am not present every day. Unfortunately, I believe that I am correct in my assumption.

Another concern I have is that there may well be less volunteers such as parents, who may have part time or full time jobs therefore can not engage in voluntary activities easily. In addition, I think that there would be some truth in thinking that working parents may be less than enthusiastic to provide their children with reading sessions on any kind of regular basis. Clearly there will be exceptions and maybe a majority of parents do provide this. But what about the children who do not have this facility and the same is limited at school?

I can not comment on whether grandparents (as I am) get involved, or whether they would like to.

I have a semi-retired lifestyle as I am still running my small business, but I am able to spare the time to attend school two afternoons per week. The first school I went to I only did one afternoon per week and I actually felt that it wasn't enough to spend a couple of hours and then wait until the next week. This happens to suit me perfectly (twice per week), not least because I am extremely interested in this activity and I find it very rewarding and I am sure that I can see the benefits of what I do, by the way that the children respond and cooperate. Obviously not everyone is in that situation, which for whatever reasons is a pity, as I am sure that there are many people around who would really enjoy doing what I do.

***

Another problem which I can only assume exists, is again based on my experience.

I initially contacted a primary school which was closest to where I live, by email, it being no more than two miles away. I received a positive response, despite the restriction in place due to Covid, but the school very kindly organised a DBS (Disclosure and Barring Service certificate) which is a requirement for carrying out any kind of voluntary work in a primary school. I then waited for confirmation of when I would be able to begin attending. As I received no reply, I telephoned the school and was put through to the head teacher. She explained that normal procedure would be for me to complete an application form and provide two references. This I did. I then heard nothing more and I know that the references were not taken up. In the meantime, I contacted a school which was about six miles away, being the school where my grandchildren had attended, but I was not personally known to the school. This school was pleased to take up my offer and although this was around November, the earliest I would be able to begin the voluntary work would have been February the following year when Covid restrictions were finally lifted and this indeed occurred. I then attended one afternoon per week and I listened to a variety of children aged between 5 and up to 9 years old. I thoroughly enjoyed this. It was exactly what I wanted to do and I would say it was very successful and much appreciated by the teaching assistants whom I liaised with.

For practical reasons it was more convenient for me not to continue at that school, but in the meantime I had contacted a total of five other primary schools within a radius of around two or three miles from my address. I received only one reply, from my follow up telephone calls. The reply I received was very positive and was from the school which I now attend two afternoons per week.

Before receiving this positive response, in desperation I contacted two secondary schools as I was also prepared to assist, being sure that there can be a problem with reading levels at secondary school level, being carried forward from primary school for even a small number of children. However, although I received a response from each and a definite interest, nothing materialised then or since. Not a problem to me, as I am fixed up and would not wish to take on more than two afternoons per week now. And I would very much like to continue with the school I am involved with and have already made a commitment for the next academic year.

I have to say that I found this general lack of response rather peculiar and a little concerning. I can only guess why my offer was not taken up in each of these cases and these are stated as follows.

Primary school teachers are so busy with their large classes that the individual teachers may not relish having to deal with another activity which they imagine may impact slightly on their teaching schedule and they may even feel that someone like myself would need to be supervised or organised. When I listen to children reading I have a list of names and I work through that list by asking for a particular child to begin with. And then each child having read to me for 5 to 10 minutes returns to the classroom opposite where I am sitting and asks for the next child to come and read. This works very smoothly most of the time and the absence of the child from the particular class activity is minimal, being only 5 to 10 minutes. Teachers have told me that the children enjoy reading to me and in particular they enjoy reading to a different grown up and of course enjoy the one to one experience. Rather a win win situation, I would say. (For the child, the teacher and myself).

Another issue could be that I was not known to the school, the DBS not necessarily being a guarantee for an individual (outsider) to achieve approved volunteer status. It has also crossed my mind that as I am a man, that may not be preferred. Although as male teachers and male teaching assistants are very much in the minority, the additional male presence could be useful.

And of course in many households there may not be a male presence.

When I am involved in this activity, sometimes I can not believe what a pleasure it is, observing a small child cooperating in his or her education. All of the experiences mentioned in this book, without being sentimental, are a joy in educational and social terms and every now and then are quite heartwarming. And of course surely proof that what I am doing is worthwhile.

All of the above is of course speculative, but if any or all of my suppositions are true, then it is rather ironic. That is to say, that someone like myself who has significant experience in education, not only via school voluntary work in the past, but as a former lecturer in further and higher education, was making an offer which was not taken up. Not to mention that I am a published author, including having written many children's stories/books and in fact done a small number of storytelling sessions in two different primary schools.

In conclusion, to repeat, it is ironic, firstly that there seem to be relatively few volunteers in state schools, who offer a free service and their time, but those who run the schools may not be able to organise themselves to avail themselves of this contribution from the local community. And of course, as a result, the children who could benefit, do not.

Epilogue

Originally, my 'Reading Project' was both a study and finding out about an area which is and always has been, a big part of my life. Having read up on the subject of learning to read, I began writing a book called How Reading is Learned, which I then had published by a company in the U.S. Interestingly and surprisingly, standards of literacy are a greater source of concern in the US than in the UK. This bearing in mind the huge population size of America (population 334 million).

Basically, I wrote that book whilst I was waiting to begin my volunteering in primary schools, once the Covid restrictions had been completely removed. But once I got immersed in this work I then began to realise that there was more to put into another book, due to what I was able to observe and also enjoy.

I also gained an insight into being in an environment where I was surrounded by young learners and their teachers. Whereas I set out to simply listen to children reading and help them to improve, this insight included looking at the whole picture including underfunding and perhaps more importantly, the understaffing in the form of classes which are much too large in state schools.

Obviously, I have written this book (and the one previously), in the hope that it may be widely read and particularly by parents and educators, especially those who occupy authoritative positions in local education authorities and in government.

May 2023

Appendix

Hen in Trouble

Quite a long time ago, Grandad was out walking by the canal. He was walking past somebody's garden which was very near the canal and he noticed that there were a lot of hens and chickens in the garden.

And then he noticed that there was a small hen which must have got out of the garden and somehow jumped over the fence.

Grandad thought it wouldn't be very good if he just walked past and left the hen there because it was in danger. Somebody might hurt it, especially if someone walked past with a dog. And also a cat might see it. Grandad realised he would have to do something about and then he had another thought. What if the hen moved away from the fence and fell into the water? Then it would never get out.

And Grandad thought that if the hen didn't get back into the garden, over the fence, during the night a fox might get it and eat it! Grandad decided that he was going to try and pick the hen up. He knew that even if he was really careful, the hen would be frightened and start flapping its wings and making a lot of noise and it might end up trying to escape and fall into the water!

Anyway Grandad walked over to the hen and he very carefully and slowly bent down so that he could pick the hen up. But he knew that he would have to be very careful not to squash the hen because it was very fragile. So he had to quickly get hold of the hen, try not to frighten it and get hold of it tightly enough, so that it wouldn't escape but also so that he didn't hurt it.

Grandad got hold of the hen, picking it up very carefully and then he leaned over the fence and put it down in the garden. The hen was probably a bit frightened, but she ran off over to where all the other hens were then she was safe.

Grandad carried on with his walk, feeling very pleased with himself. And he hoped that the hen lived happily ever after.

This story was told to classes of 5 to 7 year olds.

About the Author

Alan Pickard has been writing for more than 30 years and has worked in industry where developing training courses lead into part time and full time lecturing, up to degree level at university.

He changed course about 20 years ago and developed an accountancy business from scratch, ending up with more than 80 clients.

He is now semi-retired, attends a local primary school every week, listening to children reading and has several books on Amazon, including children's stories. Alan is passionate about reading and writing and very concerned about how poor reading skills are detrimental to young people's job and career prospects.

Being involved on a weekly basis, listening to 6 year olds reading aloud, learning and improving their reading skills, he finds both rewarding and fascinating. Having studied how the brain deals with the learning to read process, it is an education in itself to see the process in action. Many of the ways in which children and any other learners grapple with what is a very complex process, can be seen when you watch and interact with a child whose literacy level is progressing and their vocabulary expanding.

He finds the experience extremely worthwhile and because of his passion for words and what they can do, the process observed is actually a pleasure in itself.

*Available worldwide from Amazon
and in all good bookstores*

www.mtp.agency

mtp.agency

@mtp_agency

www.ingramcontent.com/pod-product-compliance
Lightning Source LLC
LaVergne TN
LVHW041541060526
838200LV00037B/1091